God
I've Got Questions

10 Bible Studies for Women

Angel Charmaine

Erin,

I pray my story inspires
you to give voice to your own.
Ask God the hard questions.
He is ready to answer!!

Love & Light,
Angel Charmaine

Speak with Chic, LLC
P.O. Box 871282
Vancouver, WA 98687
www.SpeakwithChic.net

Ordering Information:
Quantity sales. Special discounts are available on quantity purchases by corporations, associations, and others. For details, contact the publisher at the address above.

Scriptures marked KJV are taken from the KING JAMES VERSION (KJV): KING JAMES VERSION, public domain.

ISBN-13: 978-0-692-10547-4

Printed in the United States of America

TABLE OF CONTENTS

How to Use This Workbook

Each lesson consists of the following:

Let's Talk: Designed to give the lesson a sense of direction and get your thinking muscles activated. This section can be an opening discussion or writing prompt for a group or an individual.

Her Story: Designed to give you another woman's perspective. This section includes an essay depicting a real woman's thoughts surrounding the lessons topic. The essay can be read aloud or silently as a group or as an individual. Listen to her story. Her point of view may be similar or different to your own.

Your Story: Designed to give you an opportunity to examine similarities and differences between her story and yours. This section is where you share your thoughts with the group or write them down on paper as an individual.

God's Word – After reading someone else's response to the lesson's question - *Her Story* - and thinking about your answer to the question, this section includes biblical scriptures that offer God's answers to the lesson's fundamental question. There is blank space in each lesson to jot down notes from a group discussion of the scriptures or independent study of the scriptures. There is **no time limit** on the study of these scriptures. This section may take a week, a month, six weeks, six months to complete. If studying in a group, allow the flow of the group to determine how long you study these scriptures. If studying alone, take the time you need to study these scriptures.

Good Work [optional] – Designed to give you an opportunity to put the new ideas you've learned to work in your daily life. This section helps you do the internal work to help transform your thinking.

Share the Love [optional] – Designed to give you activities to share the new ideas you've learned with others. This section helps you move beyond yourself to create healthy relationships with others.

Workbook Pages – Use the pages after each lesson to answer questions, take notes, jot down your thoughts and ah-ha moments.

Additional materials needed

1. A bible – Select the version that best suits you.

2. A copy of *Speak with Chic: One woman. Ten truths.* by Angel Charmaine. The *Her Story* essays are in this book. Select the version that best suits you – paperback or e-Book.

NOTE: There is no right or wrong way to use this workbook and no set time to complete the lessons. Let me say it louder for the ladies in the back,"there is no right or wrong way to use this workbook."

Take your time.

Each lesson is chock-full of scriptures and self-work. The *Good Work* and *Share the Love* sections are optional. DO NOT feel like you must do all activities or any activities. They are there if you are able and would like to complete them – no self-condemnation sis. If you choose not to complete the activities or if you choose to create your own activities, that's cool too.

Suggestions for Use:

- Study with a church women's group, bible study or even a book club

- Use as an individual bible study

- Create a 10-day study and complete one lesson per day

- Create a 10-week study and complete one lesson per week

- Create a 10-month study and complete one lesson per month

- Use each lesson as an introduction or to preface an extended study

- Use individual lessons to supplement other materials being used within a course

- Select certain scriptures to study or study them all

INTRODUCTION

We've all got questions. Even within different cultures, languages, races, and environments, women share very similar experiences and ask many of the same questions. Some of us were taught early in life to not question God – just know there is a reason for everything. Although it is true, there is a reason for everything, God really does not mind if we ask Him questions. In fact, he encourages us to do so. In James 4:2, scripture reads, "you have not because you ask not." It states in Matthew 7:7, "ask and it will be given to you, seek and you will find; knock and the door will be opened to you." God wants us to ask Him the questions we have about ourselves, our lives, about everything, and He is ready and willing to answer our questions.

Speak with Chic: One woman. Ten truths. is a book of freedom. Writing the book allowed me to release and share with other women lessons learned through some of my life's most basic yet most human experiences as a woman, a wife, a mother and a friend. After receiving messages from various women who had read the book, I realized it would be beneficial to also share some of the biblical principles that guided me from detachment, hurt and confusion to reconnecting with and healing myself, finding my purpose and living my truth.

I purposely left out my opinions and others' commentary on the topics and scriptures within the lessons, so you can have your own experience with the scriptures. Although we may ask the same questions, the answers will be uniquely different for us all. I want you to ask the questions, listen to other perspectives then read God's word. God created you for a distinct purpose, use these bible studies to allow Him to give you distinct answers that will help you to live on purpose and in truth.

God, I've Got Questions

10 BIBLE STUDIES FOR WOMEN

Ask, and it shall be given you; seek and you shall find; knock, and it shall be opened unto you: For everyone that asks receives; and to [her] that knocks it shall be opened. Matthew 7:7-8 (KJV)

Lesson One – Who Am I?

Let's Talk – If you were invited to speak to an audience of unfamiliar people, you had to write your own introduction based on how you genuinely feel about yourself, and you had a Pinocchio nose that would grow every time you lied, what are five things you would include in your introduction.

Her Story – Read the conversational narrative entitled "Mask Off" in *Speak with Chic: One woman. Ten truths.*

Your Story – Share your thoughts with the group about the various topics, ideas, issues, lessons learned that were explored within the narrative. How does the title of this lesson "Who Are You?" relate to the narrative? Can you relate to any of these ideas? How can you relate?

God's Word – The following scriptures give us answers to this lessons title – "Who am I?"

Guiding Scriptures
1 Thessalonians 1:4 – You are God's chosen one
John 1:12 – You are God's child
Ephesians 2:10 – You are God's workmanship and were created for good works

Bonus scriptures
- Ephesians 2:4-5 – You are alive with Christ
- Galatians 5:1 – You are free in Christ
- Galatians 4:7 – You are an heiress
- 2 Corinthians 5:21 – You are righteous
- Ephesians 5:8 – You are a child of light
- Ephesians 4:24 – You are righteous and holy
- Ephesians 3:12 – You are bold and confident
- 1 Corinthians 1:30 – You are a temple where the Holy Spirit lives
- John 15:15 – You are a friend of Jesus

Good Work – Complete any one or all the following activities to begin putting God's word to work in you, your situation, and your life.

1. Pick a scripture from this lesson that resonates in you – speaks to you – and memorize it. Meditate on it. Speak it often.

2. Choose a song that connects with the scripture you memorized and listen to it often. Sing it in the shower and in the car. Play it so much until you awaken with the song in your spirit. Allow it to help you move the scripture from your thoughts to your feelings. Thoughts are great, but how you feel about those thoughts provokes you to action.

3. Write a letter to yourself from God based on your memorized scripture that reminds you of who you really are from God's perspective. Place the letter in an envelope, address it to you, put the sender as God Loves You, put a stamp on the envelope and mail it. Any time you doubt or forget who you are, open your letter from God and be reminded of how He feels about you and who He says you are.

Share the Love – Once you know who you are in God, help ensure our younger sisters get a head start learning this lesson. When you are comfortable and ready, choose an activity to demonstrate love in action within your family, community, city, state, country or the world. [**As with everything, please seek God's direction prior to doing either of the following activities. When you enter a child's life, it is imperative that you are consistent and prepared to follow through and show up and be a positive impact and influence.**]

1. Select a girls group or organization to support. You can volunteer your time, money, or talent.

2. Become a "big sister" to a younger girl. Big sisters can provide emotional support, a listening ear, and sound Godly advice.

LET'S TALK

If you were invited to speak to an audience of unfamiliar people, you had to write your own introduction based on how you genuinely feel about yourself, and you had a Pinocchio nose that would grow every time you lied, what are five things you would include in your introduction.

Use the space provided to write the five things you would include in a speech about yourself.

_____

_____

_____

_____

_____

_____

_____

_____

_____

_____

_____

_____

_____

_____

HER STORY – YOUR STORY

Use this space to jot down notes, thoughts, questions that arise as you read the lesson's personal narrative. Then, write down whether your story relates to her story or not. Explain. Why or why not?

_____

_____

_____

_____

_____

_____

_____

_____

_____

_____

_____

_____

_____

_____

_____

_____

GOD'S WORD

Use this space to jot down notes from the guided scriptures.

_____

_____

_____

_____

_____

_____

_____

_____

_____

_____

_____

_____

_____

_____

_____

GOOD WORK

1. This scripture speaks to me right now. (Use this space to write the full scripture and commit it to memory.)

_____

_____

_____

_____

2. This song reminds me of the above scripture and helps me feel the meaning of the scripture. (Use this space to write down the song's title and the artist who sings it.)

_____

_____

_____

_____

3. Write a letter to yourself from God based on your memorized scripture that reminds you of who you really are from God's perspective. (Use the space provided to write your letter.)

_____

_____

_____

_____

God, I've Got Questions
10 BIBLE STUDIES FOR WOMEN

Ask, and it shall be given you; seek and you shall find; knock, and it shall be opened unto you: For everyone that asks receives; and to [her] that knocks it shall be opened. Matthew 7:7-8(KJV)

Lesson Two – How Do I Forgive Myself?

Let's Talk – We often hear people say, "I know God forgives me, but I can't forgive myself." What do you believe are reasons people have for not forgiving themselves?

Her Story – Read the conversational narrative entitled "Fall in Love in the Shower" in *Speak with Chic: One woman. Ten truths.*

Your Story – Share your thoughts about the various topics, ideas, issues, lessons learned that were explored within the narrative. How does the title of this lesson "How do I forgive myself?" relate to the narrative? Can you relate to any of these ideas? How can you relate? If not, why not?

God's Word – The following scriptures give us answers to this lessons title – "How do I forgive myself?"

Guiding Scriptures
Numbers 23: 19 – Know that God does not – cannot- lie.
2 Corinthians 5:14-21 – Follow Christ and be made new.
1 John 1:8-9 – Acknowledge what you've done, say sorry and ask forgiveness
Psalm 32:5 – Confess to release the guilty feelings
Romans 8:1 – Do not condemn (convict) yourself

Bonus Scriptures
- John 8:12 – Change your ways and who you're following
- Isaiah 43:18-19 – Move on and forget past junk.
- Philippians 3:13-14 – Realize you are a work in progress and keep pressing forward.
- Joshua 1:8-9 – Study God's word, be strong, be courageous, be successful.

For Real Bonus Scriptures
- Luke 7:47
- Acts 17:30
- Psalm 103 (The whole thang)
- Colossians 1:21-22
- Romans 8:31
- Hebrews 10:16-17 (Reallyyy focus on 17 – it's the best part!)

Good Work – Complete any one or all the following activities to begin putting God's word to work in you, your situation, and your life.

1. Pick a scripture from this lesson that resonates in you – speaks to you – and memorize it. Meditate on it. Speak it often.

2. Choose a song that connects with the scripture you memorized and listen to it often. Sing it in the shower and in the car. Play it so much until you awaken with the song in your spirit. Allow it to help you move the scripture from your thoughts to your feelings. Thoughts are great, but how you feel about those thoughts provokes you to action.

3. Make amends with people you have wronged. It can be difficult to say, "I am sorry." However, it is a vital part of forgiving yourself. When you know you have hurt or wronged someone, it can be difficult to move on knowing you have not asked forgiveness of the person to whom you have hurt. You can call and talk to the person. You can write a letter and mail it to the person.

Share the Love – Remember, God's forgiveness is immediate, and you do not have to do anything to "pay Him back." Doesn't that make you feel all good inside?
When you are comfortable and ready, choose an activity to demonstrate love in action within your family, community, city, state, country or the world.

1. Volunteer with an established local organization to feed the homelessness in your community.

2. Organize a food, clothing, school supplies, book, etc. drive to help those in need within your community, city, state, country or somewhere else in the world where you see a need.

LET'S TALK

We often hear people say, "I know God forgives me, but I can't forgive myself." What do you believe are reasons people have for not forgiving themselves?

_____

_____

_____

_____

_____

_____

_____

_____

_____

_____

_____

_____

_____

_____

_____

HER STORY – YOUR STORY

Use this space to jot down notes, thoughts, questions that arise as you read the lesson's personal narrative. Then, write down whether your story relates to her story or not. Explain. Why or why not?

_____

_____

_____

_____

_____

_____

_____

_____

_____

_____

_____

_____

_____

_____

_____

GOD'S WORD

Use this space to jot down notes from the guided scriptures.

_____

_____

_____

_____

_____

_____

_____

_____

_____

_____

_____

_____

_____

_____

_____

GOOD WORK

1. This scripture speaks to me right now. (Use this space to write the full scripture and commit it to memory.)

_____

_____

_____

_____

2. This song reminds me of the above scripture and helps me feel the meaning of the scripture. (Use this space to write down the song's title and the artist who sings it.)

_____

_____

_____

_____

3. Write down the name(s) of the person(s) with whom you need to make amends. You may also jot down what you want to say before you call.

_____

_____

_____

_____

God, I've Got Questions

10 BIBLE STUDIES FOR WOMEN

Ask, and it shall be given you; seek and you shall find; knock, and it shall be opened unto you: For everyone that asks receives; and to [her] that knocks it shall be opened. Matthew 7:7-8(KJV)

Lesson Three – How Do I Handle All This?

Let's Talk – Have you ever felt like you needed more than twenty-four hours in a day? Have you ever heard someone say, "there just aren't enough hours in the day?" Can you recall a time when the weight of a responsibility was so overwhelming you thought you would lose your mind trying to complete the task?

Her Story – Read the conversational narrative entitled "Just One of Them Days" in *Speak with Chic: One woman. Ten truths.*

Your Story – Share your thoughts about the various topics, ideas, issues, lessons learned that were explored within the narrative. How does the title of this lesson "How do I handle all this?" relate to the narrative? Can you relate to any of these ideas? If so, how? If not, why not?

God's Word – The following scriptures give us answers to this lessons title – "How do I handle all this?"

Guiding Scriptures
Psalm 46:10 – Be still
Matthew 11:28 – Rest
Psalm 61:1-4 – Ask God for help
Psalm 55:22 – Give God the situation
Proverbs 3:5-6 – Trust God

Bonus Scriptures
- Isaiah 41:13 – God is here to help
- Jeremiah 31:25 – Get refreshed
- Isaiah 40-31 – Trust God for new strength
- Philippians 4:13 – Be strong in Christ

Good Work – Complete any one or all the following activities to begin putting God's word to work in you, your situation, and your life.

1. Pick a scripture from this lesson that resonates in you – speaks to you – and memorize it. Meditate on it. Speak it during stressful times when you feel overwhelmed.

2. Choose a song that connects with the scripture you memorized and listen to it often. Turn up the volume of our earbuds or Bluetooth speaker or car radio and blast it when you feel like you just need a break. Take a music break.

3. Try creating a To-Do list at night that outlines the most important things you need to get accomplished the next day. Remember, be realistic and gentle with yourself. Write things on the list that are do-able in one day. If you do not get everything done in the day, adjust your list for the next day. Always reevaluate your list to determine if an item has lost its importance and can be deleted or delegated.

Share the Love – Seedtime and harvest are real principles. What you sow, you will reap. When you have free time, try doing one of the following activities.

1. Offer to babysit for a few hours for a young mother or a mother with young children to give her an opportunity to have a little downtime for self-care.

2. Offer to cook a meal for an elderly woman in your life or your community, or take her out for a meal and pay the tab.

LET'S TALK

Have you ever felt you needed more than twenty-four hours in a day? Have you ever heard someone say, "there just aren't enough hours in the day?" Can you recall a time when the weight of a responsibility was so overwhelming you thought you would lose your mind trying to complete the task?

_____

_____

_____

_____

_____

_____

_____

_____

_____

_____

_____

_____

_____

_____

HER STORY – YOUR STORY

Use this space to jot down notes, thoughts, questions that arise as you read the lesson's personal narrative. Then, write down whether your story relates to her story or not. Explain. Why or why not?

_____

_____

_____

_____

_____

_____

_____

_____

_____

_____

_____

_____

_____

_____

_____

_____

GOD'S WORD

Use this space to jot down notes from the guided scriptures.

_____

_____

_____

_____

_____

_____

_____

_____

_____

_____

_____

_____

_____

_____

_____

_____

_____

GOOD WORK

1. This scripture speaks to me right now. (Use this space to write the full scripture and commit it to memory.)

_____

_____

_____

_____

_____

2. This song reminds me of the above scripture and helps me feel the meaning of the scripture. (Use this space to write down the song's title and the artist who sings it.)

_____

_____

_____

_____

3. Use this space to brainstorm and think of women with whom you would like to sow the seed of "me time."

_____

_____

_____

_____

_____

God, I've Got Questions

10 BIBLE STUDIES FOR WOMEN

Ask, and it shall be given you; seek and you shall find; knock, and it shall be opened unto you: For everyone that asks receives; and to [her] that knocks it shall be opened. Matthew 7:7-8(KJV)

Lesson Four – I'm Busy! Why Do I Need Quiet Time?

Let's Talk – "I can't hear myself think!" Have you heard someone yell this statement? Have you ever screamed it yourself? What are examples of things that may be happening in someone's life that would cause them to speak this statement? What do you do when life's stuff places earmuffs over your brain?

Her Story – Read the conversational narrative entitled "Shower Revelations" in *Speak with Chic: One woman. Ten truths.*

Your Story – Share your thoughts about the various topics, ideas, issues, lessons learned that were explored within the narrative. How does the title of this lesson "Do I even have time for quiet time?" relate to the narrative? Can you relate to any of these ideas? If so, how? If not, why not?

God's Word – The following scriptures give us answers to this lessons title – "Why do I need quiet time?"

Guiding Scriptures
Matthew 14:23 – Even Jesus needed time alone
Matthew 6:6-8 – God rewards you for prayers offered in alone, quiet time.
Psalm 1:2 – Quiet time allows time for meditation
Psalm 46:10 – You really get to know God in your quiet time

Bonus Scriptures
- Psalm 131:2 – Being calm and quiet brings contentment for your soul
- Exodus 14:14 – Be still so God can fight for your battles
- Habakkuk 2:1-2 – God answer's your questions and gives vision when you are still.

For Real Bonus Scriptures
- Luke 5:15-16
- Mark 1:35

Good Work – Complete any one or all the following activities to begin putting God's word to work in you, your situation, and your life.

1. Pick a scripture from this lesson that resonates in you – speaks to you – and memorize it. Meditate on it. Speak it during stressful times when you feel overwhelmed.

2. Choose a song that connects with the scripture you memorized and let it usher you into quiet time. It can be an instrumental or a relaxing sound. Soft music helps you to unwind and relax.

3. Pick a day to intentionally focus on your daily routine. Pay close attention to the parts of your day when you are totally alone and select a place to be your daily place of serenity. It may be the shower, the car, the office during lunch, etc.

Share the Love – Help another woman find time to be still and quiet the noise of the day.

1. Purchase and gift an adult coloring book and crayons to another woman. Believe it or not, there are benefits to coloring. It helps you enter a calmer state of mind that helps you begin meditation. Coloring also helps you to focus on the present.

2. Plan to attend a yoga class with friends. Learning yoga with others can be fun and relaxing.

LET'S TALK

"I can't hear myself think!" Have you heard someone yell this statement? Have you ever screamed it yourself? What are examples of things that may be happening in someone's life that would cause them to speak this statement? What do you do when life's stuff places earmuffs over your brain?

_____

_____

_____

_____

_____

_____

_____

_____

_____

_____

_____

_____

_____

_____

HER STORY – YOUR STORY

Use this space to jot down notes, thoughts, questions that arise as you read the lesson's personal narrative. Then, write down whether your story relates to her story or not. Explain. Why or why not?

_____

_____

_____

_____

_____

_____

_____

_____

_____

_____

_____

_____

_____

_____

_____

_____

_____

GOD'S WORD

Use this space to jot down notes from the guided scriptures.

_____

_____

_____

_____

_____

_____

_____

_____

_____

_____

_____

_____

_____

_____

_____

GOOD WORK

1. This scripture speaks to me right now. (Use this space to write the full scripture and commit it to memory.)

_____

_____

_____

_____

2. This song reminds me of the above scripture and helps me feel the meaning of the scripture. (Use this space to write down the song's title and the artist who sings it.)

_____

_____

_____

_____

3. Use this space to write the names of women you think would be willing to try yoga with you.

_____

_____

_____

_____

_____

_____

God, I've Got Questions

10 BIBLE STUDIES FOR WOMEN

Ask, and it shall be given you; seek and you shall find; knock, and it shall be opened unto you: For everyone that asks receives; and to [her] that knocks it shall be opened. Matthew 7:7-8(KJV)

Lesson Five – How Do I Stop Doing the Most?

Let's Talk – "Your life is the sum total of your nows." ~Angel Charmaine
Reflect on this quote and share your thoughts. What does it mean to you?

Her Story – Read the conversational narrative entitled "Full Grown" in *Speak with Chic: One woman. Ten truths.*

Your Story – Share your thoughts about the various topics, ideas, issues, lessons learned that were explored within the narrative. How does the title of this lesson "How do I stop doing the most?" relate to the narrative? Can you relate to any of these ideas? If so, how? If not, why not?

God's Word – The following scriptures give us answers to this lessons title – "How do I stop doing the most?"

Guiding Scriptures
Psalm 46:10 – Be still and know God
Matthew 6:25-27 – Stop worrying
1 Peter 5:7 – Let God have your issues

Bonus Scriptures
- 1 Timothy 6:6-8 – Understand you cannot take any of it with you
- Proverbs 23:4 – Stop trying to be like the Jones's
- 1 Luke 10:38-41 – Choose God; it's the only thing that really matters
- 2 Thessalonians 3:11-13 – Realize busy does not equal productive
- Philippians 4:19 – Know God gives you everything you need

Good Work – Complete any one or all the following activities to begin putting God's word to work in you, your situation, and your life.

1. Pick a scripture from this lesson that resonates in you – speaks to you – and memorize it. Meditate on it. Speak it during times you know you are trying to do God's job for him.

2. Choose a song that connects with the scripture you memorized and listen to it often. It will remind you that God's got you covered, and you do not have to do and be everything.

3. Remember what made you feel carefree and happy as a child. Go and do that. Journal about the experience.

Share the Love – Somewhere on life's journey, we learned that enjoying ourselves and taking time play in the flowers and smell the roses was child's play and not grown-up activities. We learned wrong. For many, the fondest childhood memories are shared with others. Choose one of the following activities or create your own, invite others along for the fun and allow yourself to relinquish the cares of the world to God and have some healthy, happy fun.

1. Signup and attend a group painting event.

2. Go roller skating.

3. Join an adult kickball or dodgeball league. If there is not one in your town, form one and invite others to join.

LET'S TALK

"Your life is the sum total of your nows." ~Angel Charmaine
Reflect on this quote and share your thoughts. What does it mean to you?

_____

_____

_____

_____

_____

_____

_____

_____

_____

_____

_____

_____

_____

_____

_____

_____

_____

HER STORY – YOUR STORY

Use this space to jot down notes, thoughts, questions that arise as you read the lesson's personal narrative. Then, write down whether your story relates to her story or not. Explain. Why or why not?

_____

_____

_____

_____

_____

_____

_____

_____

_____

_____

_____

_____

_____

_____

_____

GOD'S WORD

Use this space to jot down notes from the guided scriptures.

_____

_____

_____

_____

_____

_____

_____

_____

_____

_____

_____

_____

_____

_____

_____

_____

GOOD WORK

1. This scripture speaks to me right now. (Use this space to write the full scripture and commit it to memory.)

   _____

   _____

   _____

   _____

2. This song reminds me of the above scripture and helps me feel the meaning of the scripture. (Use this space to write down the song's title and the artist who sings it.)

   _____

   _____

   _____

   _____

3. Use this space to write down the activity in which you plan to participate. Write the names of the people you will ask to come along for the fun.

   _____

   _____

   _____

   _____

   _____

God, I've Got Questions

10 BIBLE STUDIES FOR WOMEN

Ask, and it shall be given you; seek and you shall find; knock, and it shall be opened unto you: For everyone that asks receives; and to [her] that knocks it shall be opened. Matthew 7:7-8(KJV)

Lesson Six – Will I Ever Stop Crying?

Let's Talk – As women, we have all spent at least one night balled up in the fetal position crying about something. What did you learn as a child about crying? What are some benefits of crying? What are some disadvantages?

Her Story – Read the conversational narrative entitled "2 a.m. Cry" in *Speak with Chic: One woman. Ten truths.*

Your Story – Share your thoughts about the various topics, ideas, issues, lessons learned that were explored within the narrative. How does the title of this lesson "Will I ever stop crying?" relate to the narrative? Can you relate to any of these ideas? If so, how? If not, why not?

God's Word – The following scriptures give us answers to this lessons title – "Will I ever stop crying?"

Guiding Scriptures

Psalm 30:5 – Yes, weeping may endure for a night, but joy shows up in the morning
Revelation 21:4 – Yes, God will wipe away your tears.

Bonus Scriptures

- John 11:35 – Yes, even Jesus wept.
- Luke 7:13 – Yes, know that Jesus understands your tears.
- Ecclesiastes 3:8 – There is a time for crying, but yes, it will end just like seasons.
- 1 Samuel 1:10 – Yes and know that you are not alone.
- Genesis 21:17 – God hears your crying.

Good Work – Complete any one or all the following activities to begin putting God's word to work in you, your situation, and your life.

1. Pick a scripture from this lesson that resonates in you – speaks to you – and memorize it. Meditate on it, and when you find yourself in moments that seem like the tears are endless, open your mouth and speak it.

2. Choose a praise song that connects with the scripture you memorized and listen to it often. Select a praise song to help lift the heaviness of the moment and allow it to take you into praise. Allow God to give you dancing for your mourning.

3. The bible tells us in Proverbs 17:22 tells us that a happy heart is like medicine. Pick a funny movie, TV show, video, something that makes you laugh one of those big, hearty laughs from your stomach. Watch it from time to time or when you feel the weight of the world and the tears begin to sting. Laughter is the best medicine.

Share the Love – It is one thing to laugh alone, but it is so much better to laugh with friends.

1. Plan to attend a comedy show in your local area with a few friends.

2. Invite a friend over and bake cookies, muffins, cake or all the above.

LET'S TALK

As women, we have all spent at least one night balled up in the fetal position crying about something. What did you learn as a child about crying? What are some benefits of crying? What are some disadvantages?

_____

_____

_____

_____

_____

_____

_____

_____

_____

_____

_____

_____

_____

_____

_____

HER STORY – YOUR STORY

Use this space to jot down notes, thoughts, questions that arise as you read the lesson's personal narrative. Then, write down whether your story relates to her story or not. Explain. Why or why not?

_____

_____

_____

_____

_____

_____

_____

_____

_____

_____

_____

_____

_____

_____

_____

God's Word

Use this space to jot down notes from guided scriptures.

_____

_____

_____

_____

_____

_____

_____

_____

_____

_____

_____

_____

_____

_____

_____

GOOD WORK

1. This scripture speaks to me right now. (Use this space to write the full scripture and commit it to memory.)

   _____

   _____

   _____

   _____

2. This song reminds me of the above scripture and helps me feel the meaning of the scripture. (Use this space to write down the song's title and the artist who sings it.)

   _____

   _____

   _____

   _____

3. Use this space to write down the titles of some of your favorite comedians, movies, and/or sitcoms.

   _____

   _____

   _____

   _____

   _____

   _____

God, I've Got Questions

10 BIBLE STUDIES FOR WOMEN

Ask, and it shall be given you; seek and you shall find; knock, and it shall be opened unto you: For everyone that asks receives; and to [her] that knocks it shall be opened. Matthew 7:7-8(KJV)

Lesson 7 – How Do I Find My Purpose?

Let's Talk – "The purpose of life is not to be happy. It is to be useful, to be honorable, to be compassionate, to have it make some difference that you have lived and lived well." —Ralph Waldo Emerson

If you knew you were going to die a year from now, what would you do and how would you want to be remembered?

Her Story – Read the conversational narrative entitled "Pain + Passion = Purpose" in *Speak with Chic: One woman. Ten truths.*

Your Story – Share your thoughts about the various topics, ideas, issues, lessons learned that were explored within the narrative. How does the title of this lesson "How do I find my purpose?" relate to the narrative? Can you relate to any of these ideas? If so, how? If not, why not?

God's Word – The following scriptures give us answers to this lessons title – "How do I find my purpose?"

Guiding Scriptures
Proverbs 3:5-6 – Trust and acknowledge God
Thessalonians 4:3 – Set yourself apart
Romans 12:1-2 – Decide to do things God's way and not yours
Proverbs 11:14 – Seek wise counsel
1 Peter 4:10 – Pay attention to what you do well
John 10:27 – Stop talking so much and listen to God
Psalms 37:45 – Listen to your heart

Bonus Scriptures *that focus on God's plan for you.*
- Jeremiah 29:11 – To give you a good future and hope
- Proverbs: 16:9 – To establish your steps
- Isaiah 58:11 – To satisfy your desire and make you strong
- Psalms 37:4 – To give you the desires of your heart
- John 15:1-27 – To be productive and bear good fruit
- John 3:16 – To give you eternal life
- Ephesians 5:1 – To be like Him and love people

Good Work – Complete any one or all the following activities to begin putting God's word to work in you, your situation, and your life.

1. Pick a scripture from this lesson that resonates in you – speaks to you – and memorize it. Meditate on it. The bible tells us that we have not because we ask not. Ask God to show you what He created you to do in the Earth. Ask God to unclog your spiritual ears, so you can hear what He says. Ask God to unblur your spiritual eyes, so you can see what He shows you. Ask God for a willing heart to do what He instructs you to do.

2. Think about and write down five things you would do to help others if money, time, and ability were not factors.

3. Answer the following questions.
   - What are my strengths?
   - What makes me happy and makes me come alive?
   - What type of legacy do I want to leave?

Share the Love – Sometimes other people see things in us that we do not see in ourselves.

1. Call up a friend or five and have a vision board party. Have fun gluing pictures of things you would love to be part of your future life. This is your opportunity to not sensor your dreams. If you could do or be anything you wanted, put it on your board and then put the board up somewhere in your house that you must look at it daily.

2. Call two or three of your closest and most authentic friends and ask them to write down a list of five to ten things they believe are your strengths.

LET'S TALK

"The purpose of life is not to be happy. It is to be useful, to be honorable, to be compassionate, to have it make some difference that you have lived and lived well." —Ralph Waldo Emerson
If you knew you were going to die a year from now, what would you do and how would you want to be remembered?

_____

_____

_____

_____

_____

_____

_____

_____

_____

_____

_____

_____

_____

_____

HER STORY – YOUR STORY

Use this space to jot down notes, thoughts, questions that arise as you read the lesson's personal narrative. Then, write down whether your story relates to her story or not. Explain. Why or why not?

_____

_____

_____

_____

_____

_____

_____

_____

_____

_____

_____

_____

_____

_____

GOD'S WORD

Use this space to jot down notes from the guided scriptures.

_____

_____

_____

_____

_____

_____

_____

_____

_____

_____

_____

_____

_____

_____

_____

_____

GOOD WORK

1. This scripture speaks to me right now. (Use this space to write the full scripture and commit it to memory.)

_____

_____

_____

_____

_____

2. Think about and write down five things you would do to help others if money, time, and ability were not factors.

_____

_____

_____

_____

_____

3. Answer the following questions.
   - What are my strengths?
   - What makes me happy and makes me come alive?
   - What type of legacy do I want to leave?

_____

_____

_____

_____

_____

God, I've Got Questions

10 BIBLE STUDIES FOR WOMEN

Ask, and it shall be given you; seek and you shall find; knock, and it shall be opened unto you: For everyone that asks receives; and to [her] that knocks it shall be opened. Matthew 7:7-8(KJV)

Lesson 8 – Do I Really Need Friends?

Let's Talk – Have you heard a woman say, "I don't have female friends" or "I don't need friends"? What do you think about these statements? Do you have lots of female friends, a few or none?

Her Story – Read the conversational narrative entitled "The Tribe" in *Speak with Chic: One woman. Ten truths.*

Your Story – Share your thoughts about the various topics, ideas, issues, lessons learned that were explored within the narrative. How does the title of this lesson "Do I really need friends?" relate to the narrative? Can you relate to any of these ideas? If so, how? If not, why not?

God's Word – The following scriptures give us answers to this lessons title – "Do I really need friends?"

Guiding Scriptures
Ecclesiastes 4:9-12 – Two are better than one
John 15:13 – There's nothing like a "ride-or-die" friend
Proverbs 27:17 – Iron sharpens iron

Bonus Scriptures
- 1 Thessalonians 5:11 – Encourage and build each other up
- Proverbs 27:9 – It is sweet to have an honest friend
- Hebrews 10:24-25 – Spend time together
- Matthew 18:20 – God is there when you and your friend(s) seek Him together
- Proverbs 27:5-6 – Friends can offer genuine feedback

Good Work – Complete any one or both of the following activities to begin putting God's word to work in you, your situation, and your life.

1. Pick a scripture from this lesson that resonates in you – speaks to you – and memorize it. Meditate on it. Speak it during your prayer time and ask God to send quality people to you who will help you fulfill your purpose versus hindering it.

2. Oftentimes, we attract who we are. If you are attracting less than quality friendships, try this exercise. Jot down a list of character traits you want the people you accept as friends to possess. Then, do a self-check and checkoff the traits you know you could improve in yourself. Be the type of friend you want others to be to you.

Share the Love – It takes one to know one.

1. For one week, choose to only talk with your closest friends via phone calls or face-to-face and not social media or text messages.

2. Plan a girl's day or girls night out at least once a month or once a quarter. It does not matter when, just plan something regularly.

3. Set your intentions to purposefully speak to and compliment women you do not know personally.

LET'S TALK

Have you heard a woman say, "I don't have female friends" or "I don't need friends"? What do you think about these statements? Do you have lots of female friends, a few or none?

_____

_____

_____

_____

_____

_____

_____

_____

_____

_____

_____

_____

_____

_____

_____

_____

_____

HER STORY – YOUR STORY

Use this space to jot down notes, thoughts, questions that arise as you read the lesson's personal narrative. Then, write down whether your story relates to her story or not. Explain. Why or why not?

_____

_____

_____

_____

_____

_____

_____

_____

_____

_____

_____

_____

_____

_____

_____

GOD'S WORD

Use this space to jot down notes from guided scriptures.

_____

_____

_____

_____

_____

_____

_____

_____

_____

_____

_____

_____

_____

_____

_____

_____

_____

GOOD WORK

1. This scripture speaks to me right now. (Use this space to write the full scripture and commit it to memory.)

_____

_____

_____

_____

2. Oftentimes, we attract who we are. If you are attracting less than quality friendships, try this exercise. Jot down a list of character traits you want the people you accept as friends to possess. Then, do a self-check and checkoff the traits you know you could improve in yourself. Be the type of friend you want others to be to you.

_____

_____

_____

_____

_____

_____

_____

_____

_____

God, I've Got Questions

10 BIBLE STUDIES FOR WOMEN

Ask, and it shall be given you; seek and you shall find; knock, and it shall be opened unto you: For everyone that asks receives; and to [her] that knocks it shall be opened. Matthew 7:7-8(KJV)

Lesson 9 – How Do I Love Myself?

Let's Talk – What do you like the most about yourself? What do you dislike the most about yourself?

Her Story – Read the conversational narrative entitled "Body, Soul and Spirit" in *Speak with Chic: One woman. Ten truths.*

Your Story – Share your thoughts about the various topics, ideas, issues, lessons learned that were explored within the narrative. How does the title of this lesson "Body, Soul and Spirit?" relate to the narrative? Can you relate to any of these ideas? If so, how? If not, why not?

God's Word – The following scriptures give us answers to this lessons title – "How do I love myself?"

Guiding Scriptures
Matthew 10:30-31 – Understand event the number of hairs on your head are important
Psalm 139: 13-14 – Know that you are not an afterthought
1 Corinthians 6:19-20 – Take care of your body because God's spirit lives there
1 Corinthians 10:31 – Eat healthy and for God's glory
1 Timothy 4:7-8 – Workout; it does have some value
3 John 1:2 – Take care of your health and your soul
Matthew 16:26 – Protect your soul; not even the world is worth your soul
1 Thessalonians 5:23 – Keep your body, spirit, and soul blameless
Ecclesiastes 12:7 – Take care of your spirit because it lasts forever

Bonus Scriptures
- Luke 12:7
- Hebrews 4:13
- Romans 12:1-2
- 1 Corinthians 15:35-41
- James 2:26
- Luke 1:46-47
- 1 Corinthians 3:16-17

Good Work – Complete any one or both of the following activities to begin putting God's word to work in you, your situation, and your life.

1. Pick a scripture from this lesson that focuses on the part of you that needs a little extra attention – body, soul, spirit or all the above.

2. Complete the Love Myself Naked Challenge. For thirty days, focus on you loving you. Each morning and night, look in the mirror for at least sixty seconds, smile and say "I love myself" messages repeatedly. Make sure you look in your eyes as you're saying it. If you want to go longer that's fine too. Focus on the areas about yourself you tend to judge harshly. Throughout the day as you are aware of that critical voice in your head, you can counter with "I love myself" messages.

Share the Love – As women, we tend to take care of everyone else's needs before our own. Try sharing your love with yourself.

1. Take yourself on a date. Get all dressed up and pretty and go somewhere you have been excited about going or go to your favorite place and enjoy yourself.

2. Treat yourself to a spa day. Get a massage, a facial, and/or a pedicure.

3. Go to the library and checkout a book about self-care, read it and put some of the ideas to practice.

4. Purchase a woman's daily devotional. These are exceptional at ensuring you are feeding your spirit God's word daily.

LET'S TALK

What do you like the most about yourself? What do you dislike the most about yourself?

_____

_____

_____

_____

_____

_____

_____

_____

_____

_____

_____

_____

_____

_____

_____

HER STORY – YOUR STORY

Use this space to jot down notes, thoughts, questions that arise as you read the lesson's personal narrative. Then, write down whether your story relates to her story or not. Explain. Why or why not?

_____

_____

_____

_____

_____

_____

_____

_____

_____

_____

_____

_____

_____

_____

_____

_____

GOD'S WORD

Use this space to jot down notes from the guided scriptures.

_____

_____

_____

_____

_____

_____

_____

_____

_____

_____

_____

_____

_____

_____

_____

_____

GOOD WORK

1. This scripture speaks to me right now. (Use this space to write the full scripture and commit it to memory.)

_____

_____

_____

_____

2. After the 30 days of the "Love Myself Naked" challenge, use this space to reflect on the challenge. Has your negative self-talk decreased? Have you become more aware of when you think negatively about yourself? Have you gotten better at countering the negative self-talk? These are only a few questions to ponder in your reflection.

_____

_____

_____

_____

_____

_____

_____

_____

_____

_____

God, I've Got Questions

10 BIBLE STUDIES FOR WOMEN

Ask, and it shall be given you; seek and you shall find; knock, and it shall be opened unto you: For everyone that asks receives; and to [her] that knocks it shall be opened. Matthew 7:7-8(KJV)

Lesson 10 – How do I find and live in my truth?

Let's Talk – How do you define truth? Is truth learned or experienced? Explain.

Her Story – Read the conversational narrative entitled "Walk in Light" in *Speak with Chic: One woman. Ten truths.*

Your Story – Share your thoughts about the various topics, ideas, issues, lessons learned that were explored within the narrative. How does the title of this lesson "How do I find and live in my truth?" relate to the narrative? Can you relate to any of these ideas? If so, how? If not, why not?

God's Word – The following scriptures give us answers to this lessons title – "How do I find and live in my truth?"

Guiding Scriptures
John 14:6 – Jesus is truth and life
John 3:21 – Truth is in the light; light will expose that which is evil and clarify godliness
Psalm 119:158-160 – Obey God's word because truth is in God's word

Bonus Scriptures
- Psalm 25:4-5 – Ask God to show you his ways then follow Him
- Matthew 22:16 – Be like Jesus and don't pay attention to other people's opinions
- John 8: 31-32 – Become followers of Christ to know the truth; the truth you know will set you free
- 1 John 1:18 – Acknowledge that you are not perfect and stop lying to yourself

For Feal Bonus Scriptures *about living in God's presence where truth resides*
- Psalm 16:11 – There is joy in God's presence
- Exodus 13:14 – There is rest in God's presence
- Psalm 139:7 – God's presence is everywhere
- Acts 17:28 – We live, move, exist in His presence

Good Work – Complete any one or all the following activities to begin putting God's word to work in you, your situation, and your life.

1. Pick a scripture from this lesson that resonates in you – speaks to you – and memorize it. Meditate on it.

2. Answer the following question: What do I truly want? Don't thing about what others want you to do or what you think you should do. Take a stand and write down the one thing you really want out of life.

3. Write down your deepest fears. Then, write down the worst thing that could happen if that fear came true. Know that God has not given us the spirit of fear but love, courage and a sound mind. When you walk in the light of God's word and His presence, you walk in courage, and even your deepest fears cannot overtake you.

Share the Love – As you begin to embrace and own your truth, be courageous and bold in expressing it. Don't be afraid to live in the light of your truth around others.

1. Invite your friends, husband, or significant other out to do something you like to do that perhaps they don't know you like to do.

2. Almost all women have something in their closet they purchased because they love it but never really had any intention on wearing it for all sorts of different reasons. Go through your closet and pick out that dress, shirt, skirt, pants that you really love but have not built the nerve to wear. Put it on and go somewhere wearing it – even if it's just to Wal-Mart.

LET'S TALK

How do you define truth? Is truth learned or experienced? Explain.

_____

_____

_____

_____

_____

_____

_____

_____

_____

_____

_____

_____

_____

_____

_____

_____

HER STORY – YOUR STORY

Use this space to jot down notes, thoughts, questions that arise as you read the lesson's personal narrative. Then, write down whether your story relates to her story or not. Explain. Why or why not?

_____

_____

_____

_____

_____

_____

_____

_____

_____

_____

_____

_____

_____

_____

GOD'S WORD

Use this space to jot down notes from the groups discussion of the guided scriptures.

_____

_____

_____

_____

_____

_____

_____

_____

_____

_____

_____

_____

_____

_____

_____

_____

GOOD WORK

1. This scripture speaks to me right now. (Use this space to write the full scripture and commit it to memory.)

_____

_____

_____

_____

2. Answer the following question: What do I truly want? Don't think about what others want you to do or what you think you should do. Take a stand and write down the one thing you really want out of life.

_____

_____

_____

_____

3. Write down your deepest fears. Then, write down the worst thing that could happen if that fear came true. Know that God has not given us the spirit of fear but love, courage and a sound mind. When you walk in the light of God's word and His presence, you walk in courage, and even your deepest fears cannot overtake you.

_____

_____

_____

_____